Little Hymns™

Little Hymns • Jesus Is All The World To Me
Written and illustrated by Andy Holmes
Watercolor by Cameron Thorp and Matt Taylor
Music transcription by Marty Franks

Copyright ©1992 by HSH Educational Media Company
P.O. Box 167187, Irving, Texas 75016

First Printing 1992
ISBN 0-929216-54-7
Printed in the United States of America

Published by

PRESS

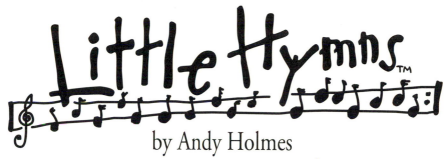

Little Hymns™

by Andy Holmes

Jesus Is All The World To Me

Je-sus is all the world to me, my life, my joy, my all;

He   is my strength from   day to day, With - out Him I   would   fall.

When I am sad, to Him I go, No oth-er one can cheer me so;

When I am sad, He makes me glad,

He's   my   friend.

Je-sus is all the world to me, my friend in tri-als sore.

I go to Him for bless-ings, and He gives them o'er and o'er.

He sends the sun-shine and the rain, He sends the har-vest's gol-den grain;

Sun - shine and rain, har - vest of grain,

He's   my   friend.

Je-sus is all the world to me, And true to Him I'll be.

Oh, How could I this friend de-ny, When He's so true to me?

Fol-low-ing Him I know I'm right, He watch-es o'er me day and night;

Fol - low - ing Him by day and night,

He's   my   friend.

Je-sus is all the world to me, I want no bet-ter friend.

I trust Him now, I'll trust Him when Life's fleeting days shall end.

Beau-ti-ful life with such a friend, Beau-ti-ful life that has no end;

E - ter - nal   life,   e - ter - nal   joy,

He's   my   friend.

Jesus Is All The World To Me